Ode to Diabetes : A collection of Poems for the Type 1, Type 2, and Ally

Lilly Kruzsely

BookLeaf Publishing
India | USA | UK

Presentation by *BookLeaf Publishing*

Web: www.bookleafpub.com

E-mail: info@bookleafpub.com

ISBN: 978-93-5744-976-2

First edition 2022

DEDICATION

This collection of poems is dedicated to my
beloved ally Jeramie.

Ode to Diabetes

We are the warriors of the world
Throughout all these trials we remain unfurled
Sometimes it feels like a roller coaster ride
But they after day, we take it in stride

Oh diabetes, you try to make my life hell
Does it bother you that I'm doing this well?

I wrote you a book I hope you enjoy it
because the truth is I don't enjoy living with you
one bit
and I will never quit

Oh diabetes, you try to make my life hell
Does it bother you, but I'm doing this well?

Sometimes you make me so tired that I hit my
head against the wall
But I am in charge and you are small

We are happy
We are healthy
We can do what we set our minds to

Oh diabetes,

you try to make my life hell

Does it bother you,

that I'm doing this well?

Our Everyday Manta

My first job is me
It does not matter what others see
I'm taking care of myself first
That's just the way it's going to be

I'm happy
I'm healthy
I'm a diabetes warrior
Everyday I do my best
And my best is enough

It's time for self care
There's no time for despair
I deserve good blood sugar
There's no time to spare

I'm happy
I'm healthy
I'm a diabetes warrior
Everyday I do my best
And my best is enough

Everyday, I make a point to smile
When I do this, my diabetes barely seems like a
trial

I'm committed to living my best life
Living and enjoying all of the styles
Say it loud and say it a while

I'm happy
I'm healthy
I'm a diabetes warrior
Everyday I do my best
And my best is enough

In Range

My blood sugar is in range today
The end result from tons of hard work
But I am worth it

I divided a big serving into two
I bolused properly
Because I am worth it

I put my health first
Without feeling ashamed of my needs
Unforgivingly I am worth it

On Those Bad Days

We all have bad days
That cause us malaise
But let us rephrase
And give ourselves a little extra praise
It's not your fault - what the meter displays
Diabetes always disobeys

High Blood Sugar

The blood running through my veins is acid
Thick just like maple syrup
Painful just like drying out from dehydration
My thirst is unquenchable
It rivals the dessert
A stream of excessive pee follows
I am dead inside

All I can do is wait for the insulin to work.

Sweet relief.

Low Blood Sugar

It feels like I'm melting like a puddle on the
floor
My entire body aches and is unimaginably sore
It's almost like something from a book of lore
Sometimes diabetes can be such a chore
It's really quite a bore
Do your best to keep doing more
Drink that juice and let your wings soar

You Are In Control

Take a deep breath and count to three
Take it to heart and say it aloud "It's great to be
me"
It is what it is, you have to let it be
Pay no attention to what others see
Let your mind be open to fill with glee
Even on those high days when you have to
constantly pee

You are still in control, you are still free
You can do this, you are the key

Kings and Queens we are a grand referee
Measuring carbs you are the ultimate trustee
When we don't follow suit, we will have to pay
the fee
That I do guarantee
The thing about the future is that there is no way
to foresee
So take a look around and be sure to smell the
potpourri

You are still in control, you are still free
You can do this, you are the key

A1C

Up and down and round and round
We are all A1C bound

I've seen the recommended numbers change
through my life
So whatever your number is, don't let it cause
you strife

Take the day one step at a time and try your best
Self care is paramount, we all need to rest

A1C is a great tool
But it's not everything, don't be a fool

Everyday starts with choices
Listen to those good voices

They want you to be healthy
They want you to be happy

Do what you can

Take one small step every chance you get
Little by little is no sweat
There's no need to get upset
Do what you can and live without regret
Try your best everyday and you'll be all set
You will feel a world better, I bet !

Insulin

It's hard to believe that it's been 100 years
To you insulin, I do say cheers
You surmounted medical frontiers
I'm so happy you exist that my face is covered
in tears
Since you know as well as I do that a cure nears
We're ready to be the cures' pioneers

Looking Good
Feeling Good

Looking good feeling good
We are doing everything we should

No one is perfect and that's okay
We have great days underway

Smile like it's nobody's business
You never have to apologize for your illness

I believe you can beat this thing
Say it with me let's sing

Stay positive and keep moving forward

Take It Easy

Diabetes can make it hard to deal
There's no doubt about that

The most important thing is how you feel
How you're doing, and where you're at

When you can, take it easy

Travel the World

Even with Diabetes, I'm travelling the world
And I do my best to remain unfurled
Packing supplies, taking my time
Sightseeing is sublime

A little extra suitcase room is all we need
Don't let diabetes impede
You can do this just like me
Pack your suitcase and travel across the sea

Take a Walk

Ten thousand steps a day
What do you say?

Okay so some days we do less
Each step is still progress

Some days we do more
We always have something to feel good for !

Let's take a walk
What do you say?

We don't need to go far but we do need to start
today
And with that, we have a healthy life underway

Make a Plan

I make a plan to help me manage
When you have a plan, it's a big advantage

It doesn't have to be big
It doesn't have to be small
It just has to be yours
And that's the best of all

The plan helps you stay on track
It's a game plan, a plan of attack

Your plan will always have your back !

For the Ally Part 1

I like being healthy, especially with you
Even on those hard days you help see me
through

Without you, I don't know what I would do
So from the bottom of my heart, I say thank you
Having you as my ally is a dream come true

You help me be a better version of me
I hope you agree

For the Ally Part 2

When someone believes in you it's a happy day
When it's you especially, I shout hurray
You are just what I needed to help me get
through I say

With an ally by my side
I feel so much more alive

All of us can use an ally, it goes a long way
With you by my side, I'm here to stay!

For the Ally Part 3

Thank you for being patient
Thank you for being kind
Thank you for understanding when I need to
unwind

Thank you for making me smile
Thank you for staying a while

Thank you for sharing
Thank you for caring

You make my world a better place
And for the rest of my life, I'll say it to your face

Thank you

Let's Eat Vegetables Together

A vegetable here, a vegetable there
My goodness, they're everywhere
And are especially good to share

So let's eat vegetables
Let them worry about their troubles

Cheers !
To you , and to good health!

In the End

In the end, it is what is is
There are things that are out of our hands
So lets lets them go
And focus instead, on what we can control

There's no doubt about it, diabetes is here to stay
And if we stick together, all of us, it doesn't
stand a chance
We have insulin, but no cure

So let's keep on fighting

Stick it to diabetes and keep fighting for the
right to be here.

The world needs you!

I'm With You

You have made the first step to a better
understanding
This is life with diabetes and we're all in this
together

There's hope for a good life, for a better life

Keep fighting the good fight
Let everyone know

Today we have better insulins that can help us
live longer, healthier lives

But that's just the rub;

We have nothing better than insulin

Not yet anyways

But sleep soundly tonight, tomorrow is another
day
Another fight for equal access to care

Another fight for understanding

Another fight for the right to live

There's always another fight

And I am with you